Golden Retrievers
Show Off

Sabrina Lakes

Sporting Dogs
FETCH MASTERS
Show Off

xist Publishing

Check out all of the books in the Fetch Masters Series

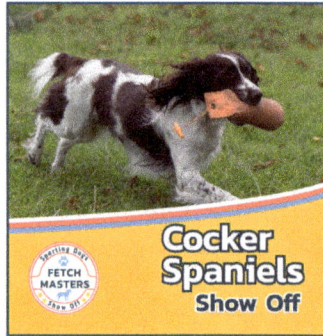

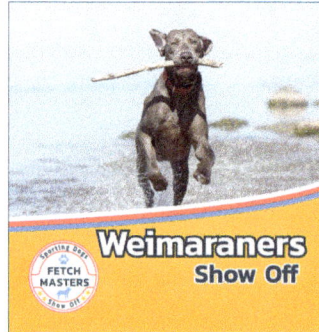

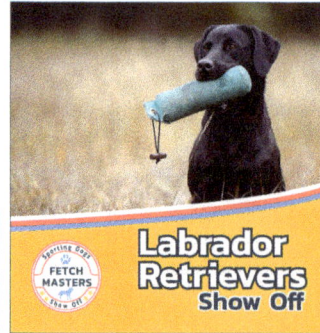

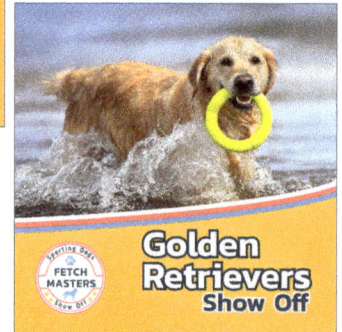

Cocker Spaniels Show Off

Weimaraners Show Off

Labrador Retrievers Show Off

Golden Retrievers Show Off

Published in the United States by Xist Publishing
www.xistpublishing.com
© 2025 Copyright Xist Publishing

First Edition
Hardcover ISBN: 978-1-5324-5523-0
Paperback ISBN: 978-1-5324-5524-7
eISBN: 978-1-5324-5522-3

PUBLISHED IN TEXAS

Table of Contents

Introduction to Golden Retrievers

Golden Retrievers are medium-sized dogs. They have golden fur that is shiny and soft. These dogs are very friendly and love to play. Golden Retrievers come from Scotland. They were bred to help hunters. Golden Retrievers are smart and easy to train. They love to fetch and swim. Many people choose them as pets because they are loyal and gentle.

Fun Facts About Golden Retrievers

Golden Retrievers have a great sense of smell. They can find things easily with their noses. These dogs are very strong swimmers. Golden Retrievers have webbed feet that help them swim fast. Their fur keeps them warm even in cold water. Golden Retrievers are known for their friendly smiles.

What is Sporting?

Sporting means working with hunters to find and bring back animals. Golden Retrievers help hunters by finding birds. They carefully bring the birds back without harming them. This job is called "retrieving." Sporting dogs like Golden Retrievers have lots of energy. They need to run, swim, and play every day.

Why are Golden Retrievers Great Sporting Dogs?

Golden Retrievers are great sporting dogs because they are strong and fast. They can run for long distances and swim in deep water. Their sharp noses help them find things quickly. Golden Retrievers are also gentle and careful. They carry things softly in their mouths without damaging them. This makes them perfect for retrieving.

9

Training a Golden Retriever

Training a Golden Retriever is fun and easy. Start with simple commands like "sit" and "stay." Use treats to reward good behavior. Golden Retrievers love to learn new things. Be patient and gentle while training. Practice every day to help your dog learn quickly. Remember to keep training sessions short and fun.

Games to Help Golden Retrievers Learn

Games are a great way to train Golden Retrievers. Play fetch to teach them to bring things back. Hide treats around the house and let them find them. This helps them use their noses. Another game is "find the toy." Hide a toy and let your dog search for it. These games make learning fun for Golden Retrievers.

A Day in the Life of a Sporting Golden Retriever

Golden Retrievers start their day early. They eat breakfast and get ready for work. They join the hunters in the field. Golden Retrievers run through the grass, looking for birds. Their noses guide them as they search. They work hard and stay focused.

Working with the Team

Golden Retrievers are team players. They work closely with hunters and other dogs. When they find a bird, they carefully bring it back. They hold the bird gently in their mouths. Golden Retrievers never harm what they carry. They are proud of their work and do their best every day.

Caring for a Golden Retriever

Golden Retrievers need good food to stay strong. They eat healthy meals twice a day. Brushing their fur keeps it shiny and clean. Regular grooming is important for Golden Retrievers. Their fur can get tangled, so brushing helps keep it smooth. They also need their nails trimmed to stay comfortable.

Keeping Your Golden Retriever Healthy

Exercise is important for Golden Retrievers. They need to run and play every day. Walks, swims, and games keep them happy and fit. Regular check-ups at the vet are also important. Golden Retrievers love to be active and busy, so keeping them healthy is a must.

Golden Retrievers at Rest

After a long day, Golden Retrievers need to rest. They enjoy naps in cozy spots. Resting helps them recharge for the next day. Golden Retrievers also love to cuddle with their families. They are happiest when they are close to their loved ones.

Fun Activities for Golden Retrievers

Golden Retrievers enjoy playing even when they are resting. They like toys that squeak or bounce. Puzzle toys keep their minds busy. Spending time with their family is their favorite activity. Golden Retrievers are loyal and loving, always ready for fun.

Glossary

Golden Retrievers Nutritious food that keeps dogs healthy and strong.

Commands Words or signals used to tell a dog what to do, like "sit" or "stay."

Exercise Activities like walking or playing that help keep a dog strong and fit.

Grooming Taking care of a dog's fur and nails to keep them clean and healthy.

Scotland The country where Golden Retrievers were originally bred.

Hunters People who catch or kill animals for food or sport, often with the help of dogs.

Sporting A category of activities or jobs that involve hunting or retrieving.

Training The process of teaching a dog how to follow commands and perform specific tasks.

Retrieving The action of bringing something back, specifically referring to the task that Golden Retrievers perform by fetching birds or other items for hunters.

Index

Keyword List

Nouns	Verbs	Adjectives	Adverbs
animals	bred	friendly	carefully
birds	bring	gentle	easily
commands	can	golden	fast
dogs	carry	loyal	quickly
energy	catch	popular	
feet	come	smart	
fur	fetch	strong	
hunters	find	warm	
job	follow	webbed	
nature	help		
noses	need		
people	perform		
Scotland	teach		
sense	train		
smiles	were		
Sporting			
tasks			
water			

Sporting Dogs

FETCH MASTERS

Show Off

www.ingramcontent.com/pod-product-compliance
Lightning Source LLC
LaVergne TN
LVHW070835080426

835508LV00031B/3471